*The only alternative
is to reverse our dominant attitude
toward the earth
and in our use of it recognize that
man is part of nature.*

— Sigurd F. Olson

Environmental Conservation Library (ECOL)
Minneapolis Public Library/Minneapolis Athenaeum

MINNESOTA
WALK BOOK

James W. Buchanan
illustrated by Randall Scholes

Volume V

*A guide to Hiking
      and Cross-Country Skiing
            in the
            Pioneer Region*

PURR'S ISLE

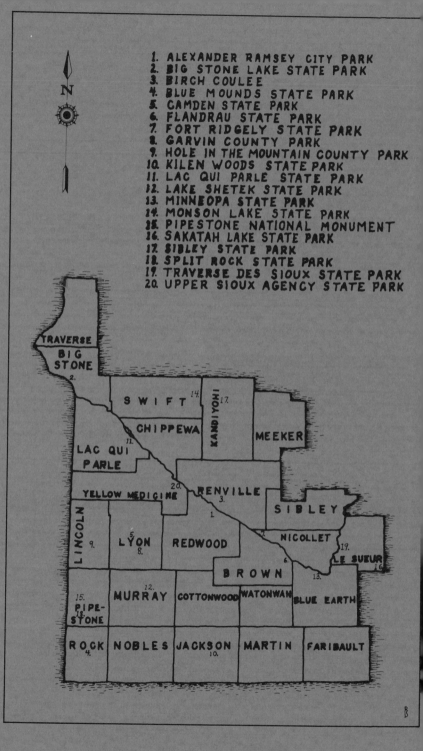

1. ALEXANDER RAMSEY CITY PARK
2. BIG STONE LAKE STATE PARK
3. BIRCH COULEE
4. BLUE MOUNDS STATE PARK
5. CAMDEN STATE PARK
6. FLANDRAU STATE PARK
7. FORT RIDGELY STATE PARK
8. GARVIN COUNTY PARK
9. HOLE IN THE MOUNTAIN COUNTY PARK
10. KILEN WOODS STATE PARK
11. LAC QUI PARLE STATE PARK
12. LAKE SHETEK STATE PARK
13. MINNEOPA STATE PARK
14. MONSON LAKE STATE PARK
15. PIPESTONE NATIONAL MONUMENT
16. SAKATAH LAKE STATE PARK
17. SIBLEY STATE PARK
18. SPLIT ROCK STATE PARK
19. TRAVERSE DES SIOUX STATE PARK
20. UPPER SIOUX AGENCY STATE PARK

THE MINNESOTA
WALK BOOK

Volume V

MINNESOTA
WALK BOOK

James W. Buchanan
illustrated by Randall Scholes

*A guide to Hiking
and Cross-Country Skiing
in the
Pioneer Region*

Volume V

NODIN PRESS

Minneapolis, Minnesota

ISBN 0-931714-07-9

Nodin Press, a division of Micawber's Inc., 519 North Third Street, Minneapolis, MN 55401.

Printed in U.S.A. at
Viking Press, Minneapolis.

Yesterday is already a dream,
and tomorrow is only a vision;
but today, well-lived,
makes every yesterday
a dream of happiness,
and every tomorrow
a vision of hope.

Author unknown

About the Author

Jim Buchanan, a native of South Dakota, moved to Minnesota with his family while he was still in school. It was in Bemidji, while in his teens, that he became interested in the Minnesota woods.

He earned an A.S. degree from the North Dakota School of Forestry and also studied at the Michigan College of Mining and Technology at Houghton. Later, at Bemidji State College, he majored in the social and biological sciences and received a B.S. degree. Jim went on to earn a Master's Degree at the University of Minnesota at Duluth where he now resides with his family.

Jim Buchanan's education and work experiences have lead him to write about his first interest, the foot trails of Minnesota. In each of the six tourism regions of the state he has found unexpected treasures.

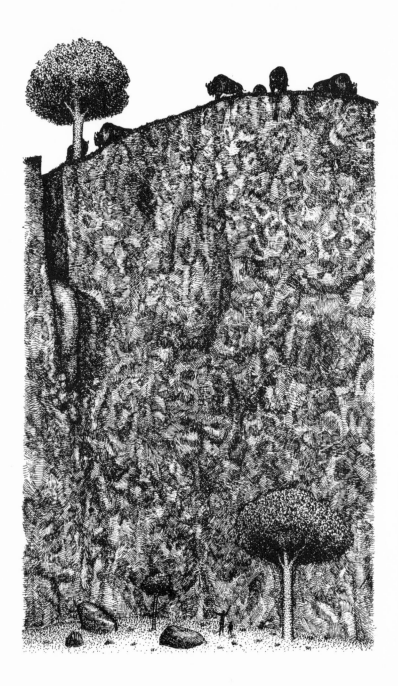

Table of Contents

INTRODUCTION

The Minnesota Walk Book is a series of guide books to the six tourism regions of the Minnesota Department of Economic Development. The regions are Arrowhead, Heartland, Hiawatha-land, Metroland, Pioneerland, and Vikingland.

The purpose of these books is to locate and describe available hiking and cross country ski trails in Minnesota. There are hiking and skiing opportunities in each region of the state, and one does not have to travel far to hike or cross-country ski.

PIONEERLAND: Geology, Vegetation, Wild Life & Human History

Minnesota's Pioneerland is made up of 27 southwestern counties. These are Big Stone, Blue Earth, Brown, Chippewa, Cottonwood, Faribault, Jackson, Kandiyohi, Lac qui Parle, Le Sueur, Lincoln, Lyon, Martin, McLeod, Meeker, Murray, Nicollet, Nobles, Pipestone, Redwood, Renville, Rock, Sibley, Swift, Traverse, Watonan, and Yellow Medicine.

Pioneerland has a total of 44, 795 square kilometers (17,229 square miles). This is 22% of the land area of Minnesota. The population of Pioneerland is 390,000, about 10% of the total population of Minnesota.

GEOLOGY

Except for the Coteau des Prairies (Uplands of the Prairies), a plateau that cuts across the extreme southwest corner of the region, Pioneerland is a generally flat landscape. It is covered with deposits that were left from the Pleistocene ice age. However, in some places these deposits have been piled up by ice movement to form ranges of moraine hills. Many of the natural lakes of Pioneerland are found in these moraines. Under the glacial deposits are layers of quartzite, sandstone, and other rock that was formed in ancient seas. In some places erosion has exposed these rocks.

VEGETATION & WILD LIFE

In the years before the white people arrived to farm the rich soil, southwestern Minnesota was a region of undulating prairie. There were many shallow depressions that formed lakes and marshland. The banks of streams and rivers were lined with cottonwood and other bottomland trees. The wildlife that lived in this environment furnished the early pioneers with an abundance of fish and game. Now, in spite of intense agricultural development, Pioneerland still has over 936 square kilometers (360 square miles) of forest land and 390 square kilometers (150 square miles) of marshland. Much of this natural area is preserved under the protection of state and federal agencies.

HUMAN HISTORY

At the present time the history of man in Pioneerland is very sketchy. It appears, however, that tribes of Indians such as the Mandan, Crow, Arapaho, Blackfeet, Cheyenne, Iowa, Oto, and Omaha moved through the region on their way west.

The last tribe to live in Pioneerland was the Dakota, or Sioux as they were called by their enemies. In 1851, in the face of a rising tide of white settlement, the Dakotas were forced by the United States government to sell much of what is Pioneerland at about twenty-five cents an acre. Besides the money the Dakotas were also to receive two reservations along the Minnesota River. Also because most of the Dakota hunting lands were turned over to the United States government for settlement, the federal authorities agreed to provide food for them through the Upper and Lower Sioux Agencies. To help the Dakota become more self-sufficient, a government farming program was started to help them make the best use of their remaining lands. This program provided land, equipment, supplies, and expert help for those Indians who desired to become farmers.

None of this, however, came out very well for the Dakota. A large share of the payment due to them was taken by white traders for bills said to be owed for goods bought on credit. The two reservations were too small to suit the needs of the Dakota way of life. The food distributed by the Indian agencies was short in quantity and poor in quality. Not many of the Indians wanted to become farmers. Only about one head of a family out of ten took advantage of the farm program. Most preferred the old ways of the nomadic hunter.

On Sunday, August 17, 1862, as a result of the murder of five white settlers by four young hunters, about half of the Dakotas went on the warpath against the white settlers. Unable or unwilling to put their forces under the effective control of their appointed leader Chief Little Crow, the Dakota were defeated in the decisive battles of New Ulm, Fort Ridgely, and Wood Lake. In a little more than a month the war was over. Several hundred settlers and soldiers were killed. Very few Indians died or were wounded in the fighting. Thirty-nine were hanged and others were sentenced to imprisonment. Although only half of the Dakotas took part in the uprising, all lost their reservations, land grants, and annuities. Practically all of the Dakotas moved to new reservations in the west. The former Minnesota river valley reservations were soon open to settlement. With the Dakotas removed, the Minnesota valley became one of the richest farming regions in Minnesota.

MINNESOTA RIVER VALLEY

Many of Pioneerland's historical and outdoor recreational areas are on the Minnesota River or its tributaries. The Minnesota River has its headwaters in Big Stone Lake. It flows from that lake across the state to its junction with the Mississippi River at Fort Snelling State Park, a distance of about 568 kilometers (355 miles). When visitors first see the Minnesota River, they notice how small the river is compared to its valley. The Minnesota meanders in a valley that is several kilometers wide and 80 meters (267 feet) or so below the level of the surrounding prairie.

This huge valley was cut by a much larger river that was the main drainage for Glacial Lake Agassiz. This lake formed from the melt waters of the last ice age. Lake Agassiz covered much of what is now Manitoba, Ontario, Minnesota, and North Dakota. It may have been the largest freshwater lake that ever existed anywhere on earth at any time. The glacial river has been named Glacial River Warren after General G. K. Warren who surveyed the Minnesota River in 1868.

The name of the Minnesota River has been spelled many ways. It was taken from the Dakota word Minne (water) Sota (somewhat clouded) or somewhat clouded water. Apparently Minnesota does not mean Sky Blue Water!

At the present time over a hundred important historical sites have been identified in the Minnesota River Valley, but only a few have been investigated or restored.

VEGETATION OF THE MINNESOTA RIVER VALLEY

The Minnesota River Valley has much of the non-agricultural land of Pioneerland. The river floodplain includes many species of wildflowers, marsh plants, and shrubs. The floodplain has bottomland tree species such as cottonwood, willow, and soft maple. On the drier, warmer south slopes, there are many areas of grassy meadows, open oak forests that are called savannahs, and elm woods. The wetter, cooler north slopes support a denser forest made up of trees such as hard maple, basswood, and butternut.

WILDLIFE IN THE MINNESOTA RIVER VALLEY

The diverse habitats that range from wetlands to open prairies and diciduous forest provide good living conditions for many species of wildlife. The hiker may see an abundance of song birds, waterfowl, fur bearing and game animals. For hunters the favorite quarry is the ring-neck pheasant, white tailed deer, cottontail rabbit, and fox squirrels.

FISHING IN THE MINNESOTA RIVER

There are a number of fish species in the Minnesota River. Buffalo fish, European carp, quilback, redhorse, sheephead, and several members of the sucker family are the most common. The Minnesota Department of Natural Resources has introduced walleye, small mouth bass, crappies, and northern pike. However, the main sports fish in the river is now the channel catfish.

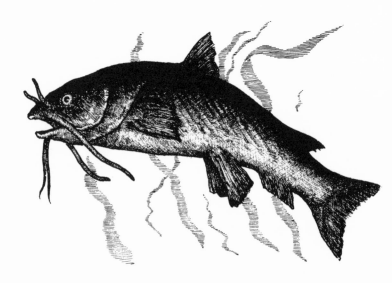

PIONEERLAND HIKING

Although there are some places in Pioneerland that seem to be far removed from towns and farms, most hiking is not a wilderness experience. There are no dangerous wild animals and the risk of becoming lost is minimal.

TRAILS

All of Pioneerland's trails are day hike trails. This means that the hiker does not have to carry a backpack loaded with such camping necessities as tent, sleeping bag, stove, and cooking gear. Day hikers, however, find that a day pack is needed for most hikes. The contents of a day pack might include trail food, drinks, supplementary clothing such as raingear, insulated jacket, gloves, extra socks, and stocking cap. First aid kit, insect repellent, sun screen lotion, lip ointment, map of trail, compass, and sun glasses are desirable items. A flashlight, whistle, matches, and firestarter are emergency items that many hikers may want to include.

To avoid problems such as hypothermia, being lost, or dehydration, never go hiking while tired, hungry, or thirsty. Let someone know where you are going and when you expect to return. Generally, it is not advisable to hike alone.

There are two basic forms of trails. One is the loop trail. As the name suggests, the trail is formed in a loop. The advantage of a loop trail is that the hiker ends up at the starting point. The other type trail is the one way linear trail. On the linear trail, hikers must retrace their steps or make arrangements for a pick-up at the terminus or somewhere along the trail.

Most State Park trail systems are made up of a series of loop trails that may be hiked from a single starting point.

In Minnesota, the prime examples of linear trails are the eleven trails of the Corridor Trail System. When completed these trails will total almost 1,600 kilometers (1,000 miles). Two of these trails, the Casey Jones and the Sakatah Singing Hills Trails will be completely within Pioneerland. A third, the Luce Line Trail will be in Metroland and Pioneerland.

CROSS COUNTRY SKI TRAILS

As with the five other tourism regions in the state, Pioneerland has a growing number of areas that provide marked and/or groomed cross-country ski trails. Because cross country skiing is growing in popularity, it is reasonable to assume that there will be more areas with designated ski trails in the future.

HIKING CLOTHING

Sometimes hikers can get away with wearing shorts and short-sleeved shirts. This may be feasible on wide, well-brushed trails during periods when insect populations are low, but it is not wise to count on these conditions. Trousers and long-sleeved shirts are generally best for most trails. Most hikers who will be hiking Pioneerland's trails will find oxfords, loafers, and tennis shoes inadequate. It is best to be on the safe side and wear a pair of well broken in boots. To wear new boots for the first time on a trail is to invite foot problems. Lug soled boots are not needed in Pioneerland and may even be damaging to the trails.

CAMPGROUNDS

There are three classes of campgrounds in the Minnesota State Park system. These are the Modern Campground, the Primitive Campground, and the Pioneer Group Campground.

A Modern Campground has a pressure water system and a sanitation building. The sanitation buildings have toilets, sinks and shower stalls.

A Primitive Campground is without running water and indoor plumbing. Facilities are restricted to hand pumps and pit toilets.

A Pioneer Group Campground is a campground that is set aside from the main park campground for the use by organizations such as Scout or school groups. The accommodations may be modern or primitive. Some modern group campgrounds have dormitories, mess halls, and other buildings. Pioneer Group Campgrounds must be reserved for use through the park managers office. It is wise to make reservations well before planned use.

Pioneerland Trails

Alexander Ramsey City Park

Trail Use: Hiking
Fee: Camping

Alexander Ramsey City Park is in northwestern Redwood Falls at the confluence of Ramsey Creek and the Redwood River. On the official state highway map its index is F-18.

The park has a modern campground, picnic areas, a zoo, and playgrounds.

The topography of Alexander Ramsey City Park has been formed by the Redwood River and Ramsey Creek. The high granite bluffs, spectacular rapids, and dense forest cover remind many of the park's visitors of the North Shore of Lake Superior.

TRAILS

There are many miles of designated and informal trails in this park. These allow access to the unusual scenic areas of this rock-bound park. One of the interesting features of this park is a suspension bridge over Ramsey Creek.

For further information write or call:

Park Supervisor
Ramsey City Park
Redwood Falls, MN 56283
(507) 637-2635

Big Stone Lake State Park

Trail Use: Hiking, Cross Country Skiing
Fee: State Park Parking and Camping Fee

Big Stone Lake State Park is north of Ortonville off State Highway 7. On the official highway map the index of the park is B-15.

This 336 hectare (930 acres) park has a primitive campground with 42 sites, a pioneer group camp, and a picnic area. There is a swimming beach on Big Stone Lake below the Bonanza picnic area. Rental canoes are available for use on the lake. Big Stone Lake is a popular fishing lake.

This lake forms part of the border between Minnesota and North Dakota. It is 42 kilometers (26 miles) in length and from 1.6

to 2.4 kilometers (1 to 1½ miles) in width. Its depth ranges from 4.5 to 9 meters (15 to 30 feet). This 5,104 hectare (12,610 acres) lake is a wide place in the Minnesota River Valley as well as the headwaters of that river.

Big Stone Lake was well known to the Dakota and other Indian tribes who made their homes on its shores. The Dakota named the lake Inyan Taninyanyan or Big Stone. This is from the prominent outcroppings of granite and gneiss that are found south of the lake.

North of the lake is a narrow low strip of land that separates Big Stone Lake from Traverse Lake. It is named Brown's Valley after Joseph Brown, one of the most prominent pioneers of Minnesota. He was a drummer boy, soldier, Indian trader, lumberman, pioneer, speculator, legislator, writer, editor, and inventor.

Brown's Valley is the continental divide between Hudson's Bay drainage to the north through Lake Traverse and the Gulf of Mexico drainage through Big Stone Lake. Both lakes are in the valley of Glacial River Warren which once drained Glacial Lake Agassiz. French explorers who traveled through Big Stone Lake in 1703 named it Lake of the Tintons (Prairie Sioux).

Humans have lived in the Big Stone area for a long time. Axes, hammers, and arrowheads believed to be over 12,000 years old have been found in or near the park.

In historical times the Red River-Minnesota River route was an important means of travel for Indians, fur traders, explorers, and settlers. Paralleling both sides of the rivers was the Red River Cart Trail system. This cart trail was a vital economic link between the Canadian settlement of Pembina and the growing city of Saint Paul.

Big Stone Lake provides habitat for many species of birds: grebes, ducks, mergansers, swans, egrets, geese, herons, and cormorants. All of this and more is reviewed at the Ecological Interpretation Center. During the regular season a park naturalist conducts a series of informative programs.

TRAILS

There are about 16 kilometers (10 miles) of trails in Big Stone Lake State Park. These are mainly multi-use trails that are used for snowmobiling and hiking. Most of the year all of the trails can be hiked.

In the Bonanza Area there are two trails. One is a 4.8 kilometer (3 miles) loop trail that can be started at the swimming beach parking lot. From this point the trail parallels the lake shore in a southeasterly direction. For a short distance it is on the shoreline before turning east to cross the park road and climb up to a ridge line on the return to the parking lot. Except for a fringe of trees along the lakeshore, this trail is a prairie trail. It is worthwhile to take the time to examine some of the prairie plants that grow along this trail.

The other trail is the 1.6 kilometer (1 mile) nature trail that loops around the Ecological Interpretation Center. Unlike the other trail, the nature trail is a forest trail.

The Meadowbrook Area trails are prairie trails that loop around the open countryside above the lake's shoreline. An interesting section passes by a fish rearing pond. The southeastern half of these trails loop through a wildlife sanctuary. As in all of the prairie state parks, there is an abundance of wildlife to be seen, including a sizeable herd of white tailed deer.

For further information write or call:

Park Manager
Big Stone Lake State Park
Ortonville, MN 56278
(612) 839-3663

Birch Coulee

Trail Use: Hiking
Fee: Free

Birch Coulee is 3.2 kilometers (2 miles) northeast of Morton and east of U.S. Highway 71. On the official State Highway map its index is F-18. This 32 hectare (80 acres) historic site was formerly a state park. It is now administered by the Minnesota State Historical Society.

Many years ago this area was the site of a village named Birch Coulee. The village and the present park were named after the small stream that is a tributary of the Minnesota River. Coulee is a French word that means a stream bed with deep inclined sides.

On September 1st, 1862, a burial detail of the Sixth Volunteer Minnesota Infantry and the Cullen Guard was attacked by a large Dakota war party. The outnumbered detail managed to hold on until they were relieved by a column from Fort Ridgely.

On the open area above the Coulee there is now a memorial mall that marks the troopers' campsite. Down in the Coulee there is a picnic area and a 1.6 kilometer (1 mile) foot trail. The trail loops through the creek's floodplain forest and crosses the creek on bridges in several places.

Wildlife use river bottomlands as travel corridors, so with a little care and luck you might see a deer or some other animal. It should also be a good place to see birds.

Blue Mounds State Park

Trail Use: Hiking
Fee: State Park Parking and Camping Fee

Blue Mounds State Park is a 607 Hectare (1500 acres) prairie area that is located on the west side of U.S. Highway 75 about 11 kilometers (7 miles) north of Luverne. On the official state highway map its index is C-21.

The park has a modern campground on Upper Mound Lake with 76 sites where there is also a pioneer group campground. A picnic area and swimming beach are on Lower Mound Lake. A small store in the contact station is a source of camping supplies.

Blue Mounds State Park is named after a cliff exposure of Sioux Quartzite that has a bluish cast in the afternoon sun. This rock has been measured at 3.5 billion years old, one of the oldest rocks in the United States. Geologists think that this rock is the root of an ancient mountain range that ran in a north-south line across the center of North America.

The Blue Mounds were given the name "The Rock" by Joseph Nicollet, the famous explorer and map maker when he surveyed the area in 1835. Nearby is the Rock River which was named after these hills. The Rock River is the only major river in Minnesota that is a tributary of the Missouri River.

During the regular summer visitor season, interpretive programs are conducted from the former home of Frederick Manfred. He has written many poems and novels about Pioneerland and its people. In addition to lectures and films, park naturalists conduct nature hikes on the trail system.

The park has a herd of buffalo. These are the animals that provided the plains Indians with many of the necessities of life.

Over 485 hectares (1200 acres) of the park's 607 hectares (1500 acres) are tall grass prairie. This prairie has not been plowed or grazed. It is a sample of what much of Pioneerland was like before white settlement. At Blue Mounds State Park the visitor can see many prairie plants including prickley pear, buffalo grass, and several species of cacti.

TRAILS

Blue Mounds State Park has about 14 kilometers (9 miles) of trails. Mounds Lake Trail is a 6.4 kilometer (4 miles) loop trail around Mound Creek and the Upper and Lower Mounds Lakes. This part of the park is covered by a woods made up of ash, oak, cottonwood, wild plum, chokecherry, willow, and planted conifers. This is a good trail on which to see birds especially in the morning and at evening.

The Prairie Trail is an 8 kilometer (5 miles) trail across the prairie to the Sioux Quartzite Cliff. It starts across the park road from the picnic area. It is a wide well-mowed trail. On the way there are large outcroppings and boulders of quartzite. These rocks, plus the steep cliffs, discouraged grazing and so preserved a small part of the original prairie. At the far end of this trail is a line of cliffs that are about 45 meters (150 feet) high. Dakota Indian hunting parties made use of these cliffs by driving herds of buffalo over them.

For further information write or call:

Park Manager
Blue Mounds State Park
Luverne, MN 56156
(507) 283-4892

Camden State Park

Trail Use: Hiking, Cross Country Skiing
Fee: State Park Parking and Camping Fee

Camden State Park is 11 kilometers (7 miles) southwest of Marshall on Minnesota Highway 23. On the official state highway map its index is D-18.

This 445 hectare (1,100 acres) park has a modern 36 site campground, a pioneer group camp, a picnic area, swimming pool, and nature center. A park naturalist conducts an interpretive program in the summer visitor season.

The part is in a hilly area of the upper valley of the Redwood River. This river is a tributary of the Minnesota River. The river is not named after the large conifer of California. It is named after a local small red-barked dogwood tree that the Indians named Kinniqkinnic. They mixed the inner bark of this tree with tobacco. It was said to be better smoking than plain tobacco.

The Redwood River flows down the east slope of the Coteau des Prairies. In the first 24 kilometers (15 miles) the river drops about 90 meters (300 feet). The result of this is a 30 meter (100 feet) valley in the park.

The hills of this park are covered with a dense hardwood forest.

The Redwood River is a good place to fish. The rapid fall of the river plus cold water springs that enter the river make the park waters a good brown trout habitat.

Camden State Park is a wildlife oasis. Most of Pioneerland's wildlife are found here, also some species which are not usually seen in Minnesota have been seen here. An example is the sighting of a mule deer in the park. The normal range of this deer is in the western mountains.

Long ago this deep forested river valley was a favored campground of the Indians. Three permanent villages were located here.

At the present time the Minnesota Department of Natural Resources and Mankato State University are working with the Council of Minnesota Archeology to investigate the pre-historic past of Camden State Park. Among the methods being used is borings into the soil to test for the presence of phosphate, an element that indicates past human activity. Another method is infra red aerial photos which can site former human living areas.

In the 1840's a fur trading post was established in the park. Later, a village developed. It was named Camden after Camden, New Jersey, the home of the village postmaster. The village is gone, but the name lives on as the name of this park.

TRAILS

Camden State Park has 14.4 kilometers (9 miles) of foot trails, 9.6 kilometers of snowmobile trails, and 6.4 kilometers (4 miles) of horse trails. Most of these trails can be hiked. In the winter 6.7 kilometers (4.2 miles) of the hiking trails are marked and groomed for cross-country skiing. These ski trails are rated as beginner to intermediate.

The Camden State Park trail system is one of the most enjoyable places to hike in Pioneerland. Its steeply cut hills, outstanding forest, and rapidly flowing rivers make walking in this park a unique experience.

One of the most interesting trails is the Sioux Lookout Nature Trail. This self-guided trail starts at the nature center where one may obtain trail information and directions. From the center the Sioux Lookout Trail follows the forested valley of a stream. On the trail there are several beautiful waterfalls. After leaving the stream the trail heads up a steep wooded valley to a scenic overlook above the Redwood River Valley.

For further information write or call:

Park Manager
Camden State Park
Lynd, MN 56157
(507) 865-5430

Flandrau State Park

Trail Use: Hiking, Cross Country Skiing
Fee: State Park Parking and Camping Fee

Flandrau State Park is on the south edge of New Ulm in the valley of the Cottonwood River. On the official state highway map its index is G-19.

The park has a modern campground with 57 sites, a primitive campground with 20 sites as well as group campground, a picnic area, and a swimming pool. There is also stream fishing in the Cottonwood River. The landscape in the park ranges from river bottoms to high bluffs above the river. Most of this popular recreation area is heavily forested with oak, maple, basswood, elm, cottonwood, walnut, and box elder.

The Dakota Indians named the Cottonwood river "Waraju" which translates into English as cottonwood tree. The cottonwood tree is a common tree along prairie streams. The Cottonwood River enters the Minnesota River at New Ulm. In the park the Cottonwood River has cut a deep valley through glacial drift into layers of sandstone and conglomerates which were formed over a hundred million years ago in a lagoon at the edge of a Cretaceous sea.

The park is named after Judge Charles E. Flandrau who on August 19, 1862 commanded the successful defense of New Ulm in the Sioux Uprising.

TRAILS

Flandrau State Park has 11 kilometers (7 miles) of foot trails, 5 kilometers (3 miles) of saddle trails, and 6.4 kilometers (4 miles) of snowmobile trails. In the winter 2.4 kilometers (1.5 miles) of hiking trail just north of the group campground is marked and groomed as a beginner cross country ski trail.

The best place to start hiking most of the park trails is at the main parking lot near the swimming pool.

Trails lead in different directions from that point. There is a one-way trail east along the floodplain of the Cottonwood River for .8 kilometers (.5 mile) before crossing the river at a dike. From the dike this trail heads south past the group camp, then turns west to end at the Department of Natural Resources regional office. Most of this trail is through a river bottomland forest.

Another trail takes a northwesterly direction from the parking lot, past the modern campground, and across the park road up through an open area towards the ridge of the valley. After passing in and out of a wooded area, the trail heads south past the park road. It then connects with the Oxbow Trail which is a self-guided nature trail. An interpretive trail guide for this trail is available at the park contact station. It is a loop trail which circles around an old oxbow bed of the Cottonwood River. The vegetation here is a dense forest of bottomland trees. This is one of the most interesting nature trails in Pioneerland. If you only want to hike one trail in Flandrau State Park, make it the Oxbow Trail.

For further information write or call:

Park Manager
Flandrau State Park
Post Office Box 412
New Ulm, MN 56073
(507) 354-3519

Fort Ridgely State Park

Trail Use: Hiking, Cross Country Skiing, Horseback Riding, and Snowmobiling
Fee: State Park Parking and Camping Fee

This historical park is west of Minnesota Highway 4 about 11 kilometers (7 miles) south of Fairfax. Turn west on County Road 29. On the official state highway map the index is G-18.

The park has a modern 12 site campground and a pioneer camp. There is a refectory, an amphitheater, and a visitor center.

Fort Ridgely is on a prairie surface of a glacial drift formation. Bordering the park on three sides are the valleys of the Minnesota River and Fort Ridgely Creek. The level areas of the park are generally open grassland while the ravines are forest covered.

The remains of the old Fort Ridgely occupies a portion of the park. This section is administered by the Minnesota State Historical Society. The Society has turned the old stone commissary building into an excellent interpretive center. In the center there is a museum where many of the artifacts of the Civil War era are displayed. One feature is an old cannon. Several maps, a diorama, and an audio-visual presentation explain how the outnumbered defenders held the fort against heavy odds.

HISTORY

Fort Ridgely was build in 1853 to protect the Minnesota frontier. The original plans for the fort called for a completely stone fort with walls and blockhouses. But, due to the poor quality of stone at the site, only a barracks and a commissary were built of rock. The walls and blockhouses were never constructed, and the remaining buildings were made of wood and were scattered around the area. To make matters worse, the fort's location near the head of three ravines allowed protective cover to approaching enemy forces.

The fort was designed to be garrisoned by 400 troups, but never more than 300 soldiers were there at one time and usually the number was considerably less.

From 1853 to the start of the War Between the States, regular U.S. Army troops were stationed at the fort. After that the regulars were replaced by companies of Minnesota Volunteer Infantry Regiments. These units were trained and sent to the war in the south, and the newer units took over the frontier guard duties. At the time of the Sioux uprising Fort Ridgely was garrisoned by Company B of the Fifth Minnesota Volunteer Infantry Regiment. While at the fort, the new soldiers of Company B were drilled in the use of the cannon by Ordnance Sergeant John Jones, a regular army soldier. This training saved the fort.

At the start of the Sioux uprising, only a handful of troops were at the fort. They were, however, soon reinforced by members of their company who returned from other assignments. Volunteer citizen units and able-bodied men and women refugees also assisted in the defense of the fort.

It was the plan of the Dakota leadership to press their offensive down the Minnesota River Valley as far as Saint Paul. The main door to the valley was Fort Ridgely. When the Dakota did attack, however, the expert use of artillery allowed the defenders to keep that door shut.

TRAILS

Fort Ridgely State Park has about 9.6 kilometers (6 miles) of hiking trails. In the winter season the hiking trails are augmented by cross-country ski and snowmobile trails. The hiking trails go across open prairie and through the wooded ravines. The same ravines that once sheltered the attack of Dakota warriors now provides habitat for many species of wildlife.

For one who is interested in the Fort Ridgely battles, there is a short self-guided interpretive trail that circles the old fort. Signs along this trail show the location of the original buildings and the part each structure played in the fight for the door to the Minnesota River Valley.

For further information write or call:

Park Manager
Fort Ridgely State Park
Fairfax, MN 55332
(507) 426-7840

Garvin County Park

Trail Use: Hiking
Fee: Camping Fee

Garvin Park is a 283 hectare (700 acres) Lyon County park. It is 19 kilometers (12 miles) south of Marshall on U.S. Highway 59. On the official state highway map its index is D-19.

The park has two picnic areas. One of these is opened for campers when needed. There are several shelters, playgrounds, and a baseball field.

This park is in a beautiful setting of deep, wooded ravines between areas of open prairie. The Cottonwood River has created this Pioneerland natural wonderland. Flowing off the plateau called the Coteau des Prairies, the river falls about 60 meters (200 feet) in about 8 kilometers(5 miles). The rapid movement has cut a 45 meter (150 feet) deep gorge which provides shelter for wildlife and outdoor recreation for people.

TRAILS

There are about 9.6 kilometers (6 miles) of trails in seven connected loops. The trails begin and return to the north side of the park road.

One who hikes in Garvin County Park experiences a variety of trails. These include walking across open grasslands, through deep forests of the floodplain, and in and out of steep ravines.

For further information write or call:

Lyon County Park Department
Court House
Marshall, MN
(507) 532-3215

Hole in the Mountain County Park

Trail Use: Hiking,
Fee: Camping Fee

This Lincoln County Park is .8 kilometer (.5 mile) west of the junction of U.S. Highways 75 and 14 at the town of Lake Benton. On the official state highway map its index is C-19.

This 136 hectare (335 acres) county park covers seven forested ravines on a long ridgeline of the Coteau des Prairies. The park is named for a gap in this ridge that was created by a spillway of glacial meltwater. The Dakota Indians named the gap Hole in the Mountain because it was the only one in the ridge. It was used by the army as a wagon road to Fort Ridgely.

The park has a small campground, a picnic area, ski hill, and restored settler's cabin.

TRAILS

The park's trail system has been developed mainly for horseback riders. The only hiking trail is the 1.6 kilometer (1 mile) self guided nature trail. The trail starts at the bottom of the ski tow and ends at a restored pioneer cabin. There are thirty numbered stations along the trail. A trail guide, available from the park office, explains the features of each station. You can learn much about the environment of southwestern Minnesota from this nature trail. The high point of the trail is a scenic overlook of Lake Benton and the surrounding countryside.

For further information write or call:

Lincoln County Extension Office
Ivanhoe, MN 56142
(507) 694-1470

Kilen Woods State Park

Trail Use: Hiking, Cross Country Skiing, Snowmobiling
Fee: State Park Parking and Camping Fee

Kilen Woods State Park is about 27 kilometers (17 miles) south of Windom on Minnesota Highway 86. Turn east on County Road 24. On the official state highway map the index is F-21.

The park has a modern 12 site campground, a canoe camp on the Des Moines River, a picnic area, a lookout tower, and an interpretive center. During the regular visitor season, park naturalists conduct nature programs from the interpretive center.

Most of the 116 hectare (287 acres) park is in a deep valley of the Des Moines River. This valley is far too wide and deep for its present river. It was created by a large glacial river that once drained Glacial Lake Minnesota. The glacial lake covered what is now Blue Earth, Brown, and Watonwan Counties as well as parts of Faribault, Martin, and Waseca Counties. In the course of draining Glacial Lake Minnesota, the glacial river cut a 45 meter (150 feet) gorge. It is the main feature of Kilen Woods State Park.

The Des Moines River is a popular canoe route from the Talcot Lake Dam to the Iowa border. After leaving Minnesota, the Des Moines becomes the largest river in Iowa.

Most of the park's forest is of the virgin oak type. Clearings are made up of tallgrass prairie and former farm lands. This range of habitat attracts many species of wildlife, especially birds.

TRAILS

There are about 8 kilometers (5 miles) of trails at Kilen Woods State Park. The trails start at the interpretive center. At the center ask for trail maps and other information.

The trail system is made up of a series of loops through forest, prairie, and meadows. Most of the park trails are wide, well maintained paths that are easy to walk. The exception is that part of the Bock Creek Trail which is along the Des Moines River from the rapids to the canoe camp. This section of the trail is on the ridge above the river. It is a narrow up and down snake path in generally poor hiking condition, expecially after a rain when it becomes very slippery.

In the winter, 4 kilometers (2.5 miles) of hiking trails are groomed and marked as cross-country ski trails. There are also 6.4 kilometers (4 miles) of snowmobile trails. Because of the variety of its trails, Kilen Woods has been called a hiker's park.

For further information write or call:

Park Manager
Kilen Woods State Park
Lakefield, MN 56150
(507) 662-6258

Lac qui Parle State Park

Trail Use: Hiking, Snowmobiling
Fee: Park Entrance and Camping Fee

Lac qui Parle State Park is 12.8 kilometers northeast of Montevideo and 1.6 kilometer (1 mile) west of State Highway 7. On the official state highway map its index is D-16.

The park has a modern campground with 50 sites, 5 walk-in campsites, and a pioneer group camp. In the park there is a lake which has a picnic area, swimming beach, and a boat launching area.

The lake is one of the wide places in the Minnesota River Valley. Tributary stream deltas have formed natural dams which have allowed the river to fill in the wide valley of Glacial River Warren. In this case it was the delta of the Lac qui Parle River that dammed the Minnesota River forming Lac qui Parle. The lake is 12.8 kilometers (8 miles) long and 1.6 kilometers (1 mile) across at its widest place. It is about 2,260 hectares (5,590 acres) in area and has a maximum depth of 3.6 meters (12 feet).

Lac qui Parle is French for "lake that speaks". This is a translation from the Dakota Mde Lyedan or Lake Speaks. One explanation for its name is that during the winter and spring, wind and wave action caused strange sounds to come from the lake. These sounds often reverberated between the lake's bluffs. The echoes may have been the voices heard by the Dakotas. Another explanation is that under certain wind conditions, waves breaking on the rocky shores gave off a musical sound. In view of this, one might wonder why the lake was not named Lake That Sings. Perhaps something was lost in the translation from Dakota to French.

Lac qui Parle was a favorite camping area for the Indians and through the years several fur trading posts were located here. The last post was named Fort Renville after its owner, Joseph Renville, one of pioneer Minnesota's most colorful citizens. Mr. Renville helped establish a mission station at Lac qui Parle. The mission opened the first school in the Minnesota Territory and later manufactured the first clothing fabric.

The Minnesota Historical Society maintains a restored version of a mission building and has done archaeological work on the nearby site of Fort Renville.

Because most of Lac qui Parle State Park's 214 hectares (530 acres) is on the Lac qui Parle delta, most vegetation of the park is bottomland hardwood trees. There are some open areas. Along the road from the contact station to the picnic area is an 8 hectare (20 acres) tract of tallgrass prairie.

TRAILS

The main trail of the Lac qui Parle State Park is the Bottomland Trail. It is a nature trail that loops around the delta of the Lac qui Parle River. The trail is along the river and an ox-bow lake which is a disconnected channel of the river. Part of the trail circles around a former Dakota village site near the river. The village site is a little more than 2.7 meters (9 feet) higher than most of the delta. This difference in elevation may have kept the village site dry during the floods.

A free guide to this trail is available at the contact station.

Another trail is the 1.6 kilometer (1 mile) trail along the road to the picnic area. It goes through the highgrass prairie on the higher slopes of the Glacial River Warren valley. There are good views of THE LAKE THAT SPEAKS from this trail.

For further information write or call:

Park Manager
Lac qui Parle State Park
Route #5
Montevideo, MN 56265
(612) 752-4736

Lake Shetek State Park

Trail Use: Hiking
Fee: State Park Parking and Camping Fee

Lake Shetek State Park is 53 kilometers (33 miles) southeast of Marshall. From U.S. Highway 59 turn onto Minnesota Highway 30. The park is north of the town of Currie. On the official state highway map its index is D-19.

The park has a modern campground with 90 campsites, a pioneer campground, and a group camp. There are also walk-in campsites for those who do not mind carrying their gear a short distance. North of the modern campground is the swimming beach, picnic area, and boat ramp.

Lake Shetek State Park is on the northeastern slope of the Coteau des Prairie. The lake is an example of a moraine belt lake. It is one of the larger lakes in Pioneerland. Its area is 1,356 hectares (3,352 acres). It is one of the principal sources of the Des Moines River. After leaving Minnesota, it becomes Iowa's largest river.

The lakes around Shetek State Park were favored campgrounds of the Indians. The Dakota Indians named the lakes Rabechy, which means "the place where the pelicans have nests". The Objibway named the lakes Shetek or pelican.

Following the Traverse des Sioux treaty in which the Dakota tribes ceded most of their lands in southwestern Minnesota for white settlement, a number of white families moved into the Shetek area. Their presence was resented by the resident Dakotas and on August 20, 1862, the white settlement on the east side of the lake was raided by a Dakota war party. Of the thirty settlers at Lake Shetek fourteen were killed and the others either were taken captive or escaped to New Ulm.

One of the settler's cabins, that of the Koch family, has been restored by the Murray County Historical Society. It is a good example of pioneer housing.

In the park near the contact station is a monument in memory of the settlers who lost their lives in the massacre.

TRAILS

The trails wind through the park's hardwood forest around the fish rearing ponds. The most interesting trail for those interested in knowing more about a southern Minnesota forest is the Loon Island Nature Trail. Loon Island is connected to the mainland by a causeway. The trail circles the outer edge of the island. It is a loop trail of about 1.6 kilometers (1 mile). A guide booklet for this trail is available at the park contact station.

For further information write or call:

Park Manager
Lake Shetek State Park
Currie, MN 56123
(507) 763-3256

Minneopa State Park

Trail Use: Hiking and Cross Country Skiing
Fee: Parking Fee

Minneopa State Park is about 9.6 kilometers (6 miles) south of Mankato on U.S. Highway 169. On the official state highway map the index is H-19.

The park has a modern campground with 50 sites, a pioneer group campground, a picnic area, and a restored pioneer wildmill. For the stream angler there is fishing in Minneopa Creek and the Minnesota River.

The Dakota Indians had a permanent campground in this park. It was near the banks of Minneopa Creek where the creek flows into the Minnesota River. This is the location of the present park campground.

The Dakota Indians named this place Minneopa which means "water falling twice". It describes the two levels of waterfalls in Minneopa Creek where it cuts through glacial drift and Jordan Sandstone. Down stream from the falls is a forested glen, one of the most attractive areas of the park.

After the removal of the Dakota Indians in the 1850's, white settlers moved into the area. One of the first settlers was a German immigrant named Louis Seppman. He built the first grist mill in the area. The mill was handmade with local rock and timber. It was patterned after an old world design. The mill ground flour from 1864 until 1890. The mill has been restored to its original condition as a visitor attraction.

TRAILS

There is a short section of trail in the Minneopa Creek valley below the falls. From this trail one can see the falls and the exposed Jordan Sandstone. It is a very scenic place. There are some informal trails among the surrounding hills, but these are eroded to the extent that they are unusable.

The main hikig and cross country ski trail is in the north section of the park on the other side of Minnesota Highway 68. This is a 5.6 kilometer (3.5 miles) loop trail. From the campground the trail goes along the wooded Minneopa Creek and passes under a railroad bridge. Beyond this point the trail reaches the Minnesota River. The trail parallels the river for about 1.6 kilometer (1 mile).

Then the trail recrosses the tracks and goes up a ridge above the river valley for the return to the campground. This is a good trail on which to look for birds an other wildlife.

The Seppman Mill Road is 3.2 kilometer (2 miles) gravel road. It usually does not have much traffic and it can be hiked as well as biked.

For further information write or call:

Park Manager
Minneopa State Park
Mankato, MN 56001
(507) 345-4388

Monson Lake State Park

Trail Use: Hiking
Fee: State Park Parking and Camping Fee

This 80 Hectare (200 acres) state park is 4 kilometers (2.5 miles) south of Sunburg. On the official state highway map its index is E-15.

The park has a primitive campground, a picnic area, a boat ramp and canoe rentals. The park is a memorial to the settlers who died here in the 1862 Sioux Uprising.

Monson Lake State Park is within the Alexandria Glacial Moraine complex that reshaped the landscape about 30,000 years ago. Lake Monson and West Sunberg Lake were formed when two large ice blocks melted when they were left behind under glacial debris. The resulting depression formed lakes.

It has a hardwood forest made up of trees such as ash, basswood, and oak. In the open areas, former farm land is now going through the long process of plant succession. Pasture plants are giving way to trees.

As with all state parks there is an abundance of wild flowers that grow in the various plant communities. Look and enjoy. Remember that state law protects all plants in state parks. It is also illegal to pick berries in state parks.

The woods, grasslands, and lakes of Monson Lake State Park provide for many species of wildlife such as deer, fox, muskrat, mink, rabbits, squirrels, waterfowl, and upland game birds.

TRAIL

Monson Lake State Park has a double loop trail of 2.4 kilometers (1.5 miles). The trail starts at the campground on the east shore of Monson Lake. From the campground the trail cuts across the woods to the east bay of Monson Lake. At the east side of the main loop a shorter loop crosses the park road to the shores of West Sunburg Lake. Although this is only a short trail, the hiker who completes it has an idea of what Pioneerland looked like before settlement. There is an excellent chance to see wildlife along this trail.

For further information write or call:

Park Manager
Monson Lake State Park
Sunburg, MN 56289
(612) 366-3797

Pipestone National Monument

Trail Use: Hiking
Fee: None

Pipestone National Monument is on the north side of the city of Pipestone. On the official state highway map its index is C-20.

There are two National Monuments in Minnesota. One is at Pipestone and the other is at Grand Portage (Minnesota Walk Book, Volume I) in the extreme northeast corner of the state.

Pipestone National Monument is on 115 hectares (283 acres) of prairie land. For hundreds of years Indians have traveled long distances to quarry pipestone. This rock is known to geologists as catlinite. Over a billion years ago it was deposited as a clay between layers of sand in an ancient sea bed. Other sediments covered this clay and sand. In time the heat and pressure of this overburden caused the clay to change into pipestone. The sand became sioux quartzite. Later, erosion removed most of the overburden and the sioux quartzite and pipestone were then near the surface even though it was covered by layers of glacial deposits.

It is thought that the Indians might have found the reddish colored pipestone in the cut of a prairie stream or in the deep rut of a buffalo trail. Archeologists think the pipestone quarries have been worked since 1200 A.D.

The quarries of pipestone have been romanticised in Longfellow's poem "Song of Hiawatha'. This poem is an idealized version of minor myths of several east coast Indian tribes. Neither Longfellow nor these Indians ever visited the pipestone quarries. According to Longfellow's poem, the quarries were neutral ground where Indians of all tribes could gather pipestone in peace. Historians say, however, that the pipestone quarries were held by the strongest tribes in the area. They used the rock as trade goods.

The last band of Indians to hold the quarries were the Yankton Band of the Dakota tribe. They gave up their rights to the quarry to the federal government in 1929. At the present time an agreement with the National Parks Service gives the Yankton Band the sole right to work the quarries. In addition to working the quarries, the Yanktons fashion ceremonial pipes and other articles from the pipestone. Much of this craft work is done in the Pipestone National Monument Visitor Center. It is sold by the Pipestone Shrine Association to aid in research and interpretation of the Monument.

TRAIL

The only trail is a 1.2 kilometer (.75 mile) nature trail. It is named Circle Trail and it starts and ends at the visitor center. This is a self-guided trail. In addition to trail signs there is also a trail guide booklet available at the visitor center. A taped lecture may be heard at the end of the trail. There are also film presentations in the visitor center audio-visual room.

The Circle Trail is a wide, paved path that can be used by almost everyone. On this trail you can see areas of native prairie, wooded areas, a small lake, and a prairie stream and waterfall. One of the most impressive features of this trail is a 9 meter (30 feet) wall of sioux quartzite. Steps at this site are the only barriers on this trail. On a prominent rock of the cliff are the inscribed names and initials of some of Pioneerland's most famous explorers. There are several abandoned and active pipestone quaries along the Circle Trail. This trail is an outdoor museum with many things to experience. Allow at least a full hour to walk this trail.

There are no camping facilities at Pipestone National Monument. For those who would like to camp, the Pipestone Kampground of America is across the National Monument Road from the Hiawatha Pageant grounds.

For further information write or call:

Pipestone National Monument
Pipestone, MN 56164
(507) 825-5463 or 825-5352

Sakatah State Park

Trail Use: Hiking
Fee: State Park Parking and Camping Fee

Sakatah Lake State Park is 3.2 kilometers (2 miles) east of Waterville on Minnesota Highway 60. On the official state highway map its index is J-19.

The park has an area of 302 hectares (745 acres). There is a modern campground with 60 sites, a pioneer campground, and a picnic area. On Sakatah Lake there is a swimming beach and a boat ramp. East of the boat ramp is the nature center. During the summer a park naturalist conducts an interpretive program.

Sakatah Lake State Park is in a hilly area of glacial moraine. The Cannon River winds through these hills. The Sakatah Lakes are wide places in this river.

Sakatah Lake State Park is one of several state parks which preserves part of the Big Woods of Pioneerland. The forest is made up of such trees as basswood, maple, and oak. The setting of Laura Ingalls Wilder's book *Little House in the Big Woods* was near this park.

TRAILS

The Sakatah Singing Hills Corridor Trail section into the park is now surfaced with crushed rock and ready for use. Now under construction outside the park on an abandoned railroad right-of-way, the Sakatah Singing Hills Trail will connect Mankato and Faribault. Designated uses will be hiking, horseback riding, and snowmobiling.

There are five trails in this park.

The Warpekute Trail is a lakeshore trail. It starts at Lane B of the modern campground and ends at the nature center. It is a one-way trail of about 3.2 kilometers (2 miles).

The Nature Trail is a 2.4 kilometer (1.5 miles) loop trail. It starts and returns at the modern campground. This is a deepwoods trail and an excellent place to see and hear wildlife.

The Woodland Walk Trail is a short forest trail that parallels the Sakatah Singing Hills Trail between the campground road and the main park road.

Old Field Trail is another short trail between the edge of the forest and an abandoned farm field. The field is now slowly growing back to forest growth by the process of plant succession.

The Experimental Prairie Trail is a 2.4 kilometer (1.5 miles) trail. It starts at the nature center and follows the Sakatah Singing Hills Trail east to loop around a tract of tallgrass prairie.

For further information write or call:

Park Manager
Sakatah Lake State Park
Waterville, MN 56096
(507) 362-4438

Sibley State Park

Trail Use: Hiking, Cross Country Skiing, Horseback Riding, Snowmobiling
Fee: State Park Parking and Camping Fee

Sibley State Park is 24 kilometers (15 miles) north of Willmar on U.S. Highway 71. On the official state highway map its index is F-16.

This 550 hectare (1,360 acres) park has a modern 85 site campground, a pioneer campground, and a children's camp. There is a large picnic area and a swimming beach on Andrews Lake. Boats and canoes are available for rental.

The park is named after Henry Hastings Sibley, general agent for the American Fur Company, a delegate from the Minnesota Territory in the United States Congress, and the first governor of the State of Minnesota. In 1862 he commanded the military forces which put down the Sioux Uprising. In 1863 he led a military expedition into the Dakota Territory. He later became a regent of the University of Minnesota and the president of the Minnesota Historical Society.

The area around the park is said to have been Sibley's favorite hunting ground.

The complex moraine topography in the park was created by the movement of three separate ice lobes that crossed the region in the last ice age. Mount Tom is the highest hill in this moraine area. In the past the Dakota Indians used Mount Tom as a signal station and a lookout.

Sibley State Park is covered with a dense virgin hardwood forest. Among the trees found in the park are oak, maple, ironwood, aspen, and birch. The only native conifer is the eastern red cedar. This tree is found mainly on the slopes of the hills. Many of the novelty items sold in Minnesota visitor shops are made from red cedar wood. In pioneer days the cedar trees were a source of fenceposts. Red cedar berries are a favorite food of finch, cedar waxwing, blue jay, wild turkey, and quail. Deer like to browse on its twigs and foliage.

TRAILS

The park has 6.4 kilometers (4 miles) of foot trails, 8 kilometers (5 miles) of saddle trails, 9.6 kilometers (6 miles) of snowmobile trails, and 4.8 kilometers (3 miles) of cross country ski trails. Except for places where these trails cross wet areas, they can be hiked. The most popular trail in the park is the Mount Tom Trail. It is a 4 kilometer (2.5 miles) loop trail. It starts at the east end of the main campground and goes uphill around Mount Tom and back. There are several scenic overlooks from this trail.

Other loop trails start at the trail center. These trails are made up of three loops that range from 1.6 kilometers (1 mile) to 4.8 kilometers (3 miles). Sections of these trails are quite hilly, and there are scenic overlooks on some high points of the trails. Other parts of these trails pass through low areas that might be wet after a period of rainy weather. Check with the park staff on the condition of these trails.

For further information write or call:

Park Manager
Sibley State Park
New London, MN 56273
(612) 354-2443

Split Rock Creek State Park

Trail Use: Hiking
Fee: State Park Parking and Camping Fee

Split Rock Creek State Park is located 19 kilometers (12 miles) south of Pipestone on Minnesota Highway 23.

This 91 hectare (225 acres) recreation area has a modern 17 site campground, a pioneer camp, a picnic area, and a swimming beach. For most visitors the main attraction is Split Rock Lake. It was created by the damming of Split Rock Creek. It is the only recreational lake in this part of Pioneerland. The lake offers sports fishing for bullheads, perch, and pike. In recent years winter fishing through the ice has drawn the attention of area anglers.

The park is named after outcroppings of sioux quartzite that can be seen along Split Rock Creek. This rock was originally a soft sandstone, but time, heat, pressure, and chemical action have changed it into quartzite, one of the hardest rocks.

Much of the park area was cropped or grazed before becoming a state park. There were no trees. Soon after the development of the park was started, elm and ash were planted in the picnic and camping areas to provide shade. On the west side of the road to the campground is a 12 hectare (30 acres) plot of tallgrass prairie. It has never been plowed or grazed.

At the present time not much is known about pre-historic man in the park area. Because the park is only a short distance from the pipestone quarries, many people feel that Indians may have camped near Split Rock Creek on their way to or from quarrying pipestone.

There is a .8 kilometer (.5 mile) one-way foot trail along the shoreline of Split Rock Lake from the primitive campground on the north end of the lake, to the dam on the south end of the lake. This is a good trail on which to see water birds — especially during the spring and fall migration periods. Birds gather here because this is the only lake in the area.

For further information write or call:

Park Manager
Split Rock Creek State Park
Route 2
Jasper, MN 56144
(507) 348-7908

Traverse des Sioux State Park

Trail Use: Hiking
Fee: State Park Parking Fee

This 138 hectare (340 acres) state park is on the east side of U.S. Highway 169 about 3.2 kilometers (2 miles) north of St. Peter. On the official state highway map its index is I-19.

The park has a picnic area, stream fishing in the Minnesota River, and is the site of one of the first settlements in Minnesota.

The park is in a several layer terrace of Glacial River Warren. Because the topography here ranges from valley ridge to floodplain, the vegetation varies from grassland to bottomland hardwood forest that is typical of the Minnesota River Valley.

The Dakota Indians called this place Oliyu-wege which means the place of crossing, a ford.

When the French arrived, they named the place Traverse des Sioux, or, "Crossing of the Sioux". It was the site of many temporary fur trading posts.

About the year 1820 Louis Provencelle set up a permanent trading post at Traverse des Sioux. In time a small village of fur trade employees and their families grew around the post. In 1843 the first of several missions to the Dakota Indians was established in the village. Later Traverse des Sioux became the headquarters of the Columbia Fur Company.

Traverse des Sioux has a very important place in Minnesota history because it was there on July 23, 1851, that thirty-five Dakota Indian Chiefs signed away tribal rights to twenty-four million acres of southern Minnesota.

Ater the treaty was signed, the Traverse des Sioux Land Company organized the village of Traverse des Sioux. By the year 1853, the village had over seventy buildings. It was the temporary Nicollet county seat. However, when neighboring St. Peter became the permanent county seat, Traverse des Sioux soon became a ghost town. In a few years nothing remained except cellar depressions.

STATE WAYSIDE AND PARK

The Traverse des Sioux State Wayside is .4 kilometer (.25 mile) north of the entrance to the State Park. It is on the west side of U.S. Highway 169. In 1906, the state acquired .93 hectare (2.3 acres) for this State Wayside. In 1914 a bronze plaque commemorating the treaty site was placed on a large granite boulder. The boulder was supposed to have been used at the treaty ceremonies as a table for the exchange of gifts. In 1931, the state park department moved a cabin similar to that of Louis Provencelle's into the Wayside as a visitor attraction.

In the year 1931, Traverse des Sioux State Park was established across the highway from the State Wayside.

TRAILS

The village of Traverse des Sioux Trail is on the upper terrace of the park near the picnic area. This is an .8 kilometer (.5 mile) historic trail through the Traverse des Sioux village site. Signs on this trail locate and describe some of the prominent buildings that used to be located in this now empty field. Other signs tell where the steamboat landing and the village spring were located.

The hiking trails are on the floodplain of the Minnesota River. These trails are mainly forested trails through the Minnesota River bottomlands. These trails can be very wet in the spring and after a heavy summer rain.

Wild river bottoms like the Minnesota River at Traverse des Sioux State Park provide excellent habitat for many species of wildlife. While walking the trails, this writer saw a fox and heard a bobcat. There were tracks of many other animals on the soft ground.

For further information write or call:

Park Manager
Traverse des Sioux State Park
Route 1, Box 305
St. Peter, MN 56082
(507) 931-4452

Upper Sioux Agency State Park

Trail Use: Hiking, Cross Country Skiing, Snowmobiling
Fee: State Park Parking Fee

Upper Sioux Agency State Park is 6.4 kilometers (4 miles) southeast of Granite Falls on State Highway 67. On the official state highway map the index is E-17.

This 445 hectare (1,100 acres) park has two picnic areas, a visitor center, and a boat ramp on the Minnesota River.

Upper Sioux Agency State Park is on a plateau of glacial drift between the valleys of the Minnesota and Yellow Medicine Rivers. Yellow Medicine is a translation from the Dakota Pezhihutazizi kapi or Yellow Medicine Diggings. The yellow medicine was the roots of the moonseed which was used for medicinal purposes. It grows profusely in the area.

Much of the Upper Sioux Agency State Park is former farmland. About 148 hectares (367 acres) of the park's 445 hectares (1,100 acres) are elm and oak woods on hills above the Minnesota and Yellow Medicine Rivers. On the upper slopes of the plateau where the land was too steep or rocky to farm, there is still over 40 hectares (100 acres) of virgin tallgrass prairie.

As part of the Minnesota Valley Dakota Indian Reservation, the Uper Sioux Agency served to distribute food and other supplies to the Indians. Another function of the Agency was to provide vocational education to the Indians who wished to learn farming, carpentry, and other skills designed to help the Indians live in the modern world.

At the start of the Sioux Uprising, the agency staff, guided by a Dakota farmer named John Other Day, fled the Agency, and the rebellious Dakotas burned the agency buildings. After the uprising was suppressed, the Minnesota River Valley reservations were taken from the Dakotas and opened up to homesteaders. One of these homesteaders, George Olds, acquired the Upper Sioux Agency site. He rebuilt the main building and farmed the land. The restored building is now being developed as an interpretetive center by the Minnesota Historical Society.

TRAILS

Upper Sioux Agency State Park has about 9.6 kilometers (6 miles) of trails. Three of the trails are called Agency Branch Trails. They parallel the park road from the old Agency buildings to a scenic overlook. The North Branch Agency Trail is on the north slope of the plateau. A good part of this trail is through hardwood forest. The South Branch is on the south slope of the plateau and also mainly a forest trail. The Middle Branch Agency Trail borders the park road and is an open prairie trail. These three Branch Agency Trails all terminate at the overlook. You may take one trail to the overlook and return on another. Each of these trails is about 1.6 kilometers (1 mile) one way.

The Nature Trail is a 1.8 kilometer (1.1 mile) loop trail. It begins near the old agency buildings. This is a self-guided trail through a deciduous forest communmity with some openings in the forest cover. Trees and other plants are identified by signs. There are some views of the Minnesota River Valley from this trail.

John Other Day Trail is the trail used by namesake John Other Day to rescue the Agency staff. The trail starts south of the upper picnic area and follows the Minnesota Highway 67 for .4 kilometer (.25 mile) before turning south and down hill through woods and grasslands to the valley of the Yellow Medicine River. After .8 kilometer (.5 mile) along the river, the John Other Day Trail joins the Yellow Medicine Trail.

The Yellow Medicine Trail starts south of the upper picnic area and heads downhill through an open area into the wooded valley of the Yellow Medicine River. The trail crosses the river on a bridge and follows the river downstream for about .8 kilometer (.5 mile) before making a loop up to an overlook above the Yellow Medicine River Valley.

The Yellow Medicine River Valley in the upper Sioux Agency State Park is one of the most scenic places in Pioneerland. Because of the historical significance of this park, the natural features here may be overlooked by many visitors.

For further information write or call:

Park Manager
Upper Sioux Agency State Park
Route 2, Box 92
Granite Falls, MN 56241
(612) 564-4777

Notes

Notes

Suggested Reading

The Magic of Walking by Aaron Sussman and Ruth Goode, Simon and Schuster.

Creative Walking for Physical Fitness by Harry J. Johnson, M.D., Grosset and Dunlap.

Audubon Society Field Guide to North American Birds, Eastern Region by John Bull and John Farrand, Alfred A. Knopf.

Northlands Wild Flowers, A Guide to the Minnesota Region by John Moyle and Evelyn W. Moyle, University of Minnesota Press.

Minnesota's Rocks and Waters by George M. Schwartz and George A. Thiel, University of Minnesota Press.

The Mammals of Minnesota by Harvey L. Gunderson and James R. Beer, University of Minnesota Press.

A Field Guide to Trees and Shrubs by George Petrides, Houghton, Mifflin

The Outdoor Eye, A Sportsman's Guide by Charles Elliott, Outdoor Life, Funk and Wagnalls.

Grazing, The Minnesota Wild Eater's Food Book by Mike Link, Voyageur Press.

The Streams and Rivers of Minnesota by Thomas F. Waters, University of Minnesota Press.

MINNESOTA
PIONEERLAND
REGION

$4.50

WITHDRAWN